STINKING SPACE JOKES

Compiled by Karen King

TOP THAT! **Kids**™

Copyright © 2004 Top That! Publishing plc,
Tide Mill Way, Woodbridge, Suffolk, IP12 1AP, UK
Top That! is a Registered Trademark of Top That! Publishing plc.
www.topthatpublishing.com

What songs
do the planets like
to sing?

Nep-tunes.

What do you call a spaceship with
a faulty air-conditioning unit?

A frying saucer.

How many balls of string
does it take to reach the moon?

One if it's long enough.

Why did the old astronaut put
wheels on his rocking chair?

Because he wanted to rock and roll.

How can an astronaut make a pair of trousers last?

By wearing the jacket first.

Did you hear about the alien who threw away his shoes because they were sticking their tongues out at him?

Why did the astronaut wear yellow trousers?

His white ones were at the cleaners.

What do you get if you cross a popstar with an extra-terrestrial?

Kym Martian.

Why didn't
the astronaut get burnt
when he landed on the Sun?

He went at night.

Why did the boy become an
astronaut?

Because he was no Earthly good.

What's the best
way to talk to a Martian?

Long distance.

Why do the stars come out at night?

They have no other place to go.

What kind of light
goes round Earth?

A satel-lite.

What do
aliens wear to posh weddings?

Space suits.

What do you call a crazy spaceman?

An astronut.

What do astronauts have
their drinks in?

Sunglasses.

What is the centre of gravity?

The letter v.

What did
the metric alien say?

Take me to your litre.

If a flying saucer
is an aircraft, what is a
flying broomstick?

A witchcraft.

What alien has six legs, two
bodies, ten eyes, black teeth,
three noses and five arms?

An extremely ugly one.

What kind of star
wears sunglasses?

A pop star.

What would you do if an alien
spaceship crashed into your front door?

Run out through the back door.

How can you tell if a giant
alien is under your bed?

Your nose touches the ceiling.

What cartoon
character comes
from outer space?

Pluto.

What's green, has one eyebrow, plays the guitar and lives on Mars?

Alien Gallagher.

What did the astronaut cook for his lunch?

An unidentified frying object.

How do you get a baby astronaut to sleep?

You rock-et.

What did the boy star say to the girl star?

I really glow for you.

Why did the astronaut put some birdseed in his shoes?

Because he had pigeon toes.

Why did the headless alien go to the psychiatrist?

Because he wasn't all there.

Did you hear about the man who was captured by extra-terrestrial teddy bears?

He had a close encounter of the furred kind.

How does an astronaut shave?

With a laser blade.

What do astronauts wear to keep warm?

Apollo-necks.

Why don't they run out of drinking cups in space?

They have the Big Dipper.

What kind of ticks do you find on the moon?

Lunarticks.

What holds the moon up?

Moon beams.

When is
a window like a star?

When it's a skylight.

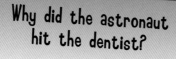

Why did the astronaut
hit the dentist?

Because he got on his nerves.

How did the astronaut stop
the cold going to his chest?

He tied a knot in his neck.

Why did the doctor write on the
astronaut's toes?

He was adding a footnote.

Astronaut: Doctor, I've got double vision. How can I cure it?

Doctor: Go around with one eye shut.

Astronaut: Doctor, every night I dream that there are horrible green aliens under my bed. What should I do?

Doctor: Saw the legs off your bed.

What sweets do astronauts eat in space?

Mars-mallows.

Where do Martians go for a drink?

To a Mars bar.

What's the name of the peace troops on Mars?

Green Peace.

If Martians live on Mars and Venusians live on Venus, who lives on Pluto?

Fleas.

What planet can we always see without a telescope?

Planet Earth.

Why couldn't the astronaut land on the moon?

It was full.

What kind of poem can you find in outer space?

Uni-verse.

What are flying saucers used for?

To hold flying cups.

Why is the moon bald?

It has no 'air.

What time do astronauts eat lunch?

At launch time.

What stars go to jail?

Shooting stars.

Why did Santa's sleigh move so fast?

It was pulled by a comet.

How do we know that Saturn has been married more than once?

He's got lots of rings.

Why do astronauts like to do subtraction?

They are always ready to countdown.

What do you feed an angry alien with a ray gun?

Whatever it wants.

Why did
the alien take his nose apart?

To see how it runs.

What chocolate bars do astronauts eat?

Milky Ways and Mars bars.

What kind of
cartoons do Martians watch?

Lunar tunes.

What do
you get when you cross
a comet with a guppy?

A star fish.

Where do astronauts leave
their spaceships?

At parking meteors.

Why wouldn't the astronaut let
Saturn use his bath?

Because he'd leave a ring around it.

What kind
of bulbs should you
plant on the moon?

Light bulbs.

What do astronauts serve their food on?

Flying saucers.

What only works when it's fired?

A rocket.

What do you get if you cross a galaxy with a toad?

Star warts.

How can you make your money go further?

Send it up in a rocket.

What's the difference between an alien and a biscuit?

You can't dip an alien in your tea.

How did the stupid alien burn his neck?

Ironing the collar of his shirt.

What's the best way to see a flying saucer?

Trip up a waiter.

How does the solar system hold up its trousers?

With an Asteroid Belt.

How did the cow celebrate his goal in the interplanetary football match?

He jumped over the moon!

What do you call a flea that lives in an alien's ear?

A space invader.

Why do Martians have two antennae on their heads?

So they can receive in stereo.

What goes through water and doesn't get wet?

A shaft of sunlight.

Are the
moon and Earth
good friends?

Yes, they've been going around
together for years.

Who starred in the Martian
version of King Kong?

The Green Giant.

What do aliens eat after
having their teeth out?

The dentist.

What did
the Martian say to the
petrol pump?

Take your finger out of your ear
when I'm talking to you.

Why did the astronaut
eat the candle?

He wanted a light snack.

How do spacemen pass the
time on long trips?

They play astronauts and crosses.

How did Saturn get married?

In a multi-ring ceremony.

Why did the huge, green, double-headed
alien wear sunglasses on the beach?

So no one would recognise him.

Did you hear about the alien who ate bits of metal every night?

It was his staple diet.

What's a Martian's normal eyesight?

20-20-20.

What do you call a space magician?

A flying sorcerer.

Why did the astronauts walk out of the bar on the moon?

It had no atmosphere.

What did
the astronaut eat for
a quick snack?

Runner beans.

Why are Martians green?

Because they forgot to take
their travel sickness tablets.

What happened to the astronaut
who swallowed a door knob?

It turned his stomach.

Where do astronauts
keep their sandwiches?

In a launch box.

When is the
moon heaviest?

When it's full.

What do you get if you
cross a rocket with a kangaroo?

A space shuttle that makes
short hops.

How many Martians can you fit in an
empty spaceship?

One. After that it isn't empty anymore.

On which
day was the first
moon landing?

Moon day.

What did it say on the alien's school report?

This pupil's work is out of this world.

Did you hear about the astronaut who never cleaned his glasses?

He gave everyone filthy looks.

What's green and extremely dangerous?

A Martian with a hand grenade.

Where do aliens go to see a film?

Cine-Mars.

Astronaut 1:
What has a green and yellow striped body, six hairy legs and great big eyes on stalks?

Astronaut 2: I don't know. Why?

Astronaut 1: One's just crawled up the leg of your space suit.

Did you hear about the alien who did bird impressions?

He ate worms.

Why did Captain Kirk go into the ladies' toilets?

To boldly go where no other man has gone before.

Astronaut: Doctor, I'm having trouble with my breathing.

Doctor: Well, we must give you something to stop that.

What's mad
and goes to the moon?

A loony module.

Martian mum: You can't come in
unless your feet are clean.

Little Martian: My feet are clean,
it's my shoes that are dirty.

Alien 1: What do you mean
by telling everyone I'm an idiot?

Alien 2: Sorry, I didn't know it
was supposed to be a secret.

What's green, has two antennae
on its head and goes up and down?

A Martian in a lift.

Astronaut: Doctor, my hair keeps falling out. Can you give me something to keep it in?

Doctor: Here's a paper bag.

Billy: What's the difference between an alien and a pillar box?

Mick: I don't know.

Billy: It's no good sending you to post a letter then.

What kind of saddle does a space horse wear?

A saddle-lite.

What happened to the Martian who ate a lump of sugar?

He got a lump in his throat.

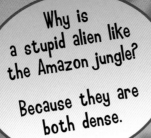

Why is
a stupid alien like
the Amazon jungle?

Because they are
both dense.

Did you hear about the astronaut
whose kitchen was so small he
could only keep condensed milk?

Why did the astronaut stand on his head?

To turn things over in his mind.

What do
you call a Martian who
murders his father and mother?

An orphan.

Astronaut 1: I've just seen an alien with no nose.

Astronaut 2: Really? How does it smell?

Astronaut 1: Terrible.

What do you call an alien with a spaceship on his head?

Dead.

What did the astronaut do when he wore his trousers out?

Wore them in again.

An astronaut went swimming and all his clothes were stolen. What did he come home in?

The dark.

Why was the thirsty alien hanging around the computer?

He was looking for the space bar!

Why didn't the Dog Star laugh at the joke?

It was Sirius.

Why did the astronaut jump out of the window?

To try his new jumpsuit.

Astronaut: Doctor, I think I'm shrinking.

Doctor: Well, you'll just have to be a little patient.

Astronaut 1: We're going to be very tired on April Fools' Day.

Astronaut 2: Why?

Astronaut 1: Because we'll have had a 31-day March.

Doctor: You must take four teaspoons of this medicine before every meal.

Astronaut: But I've only got three teaspoons.

What do you call a Martian in the desert?

Lost.

Why is a moon rock tastier than an earth rock?

Because it is a little meatier (meteor).

What do you call a meteor that thinks that two and two is five?

Meteowrong.

Why did the alien put a net over his head?

Because he wanted to catch his breath.

Did you hear about the horrible, hairy alien who did farmyard impressions?

He didn't do the noises, he just made the smells.

How do you stop an alien from screaming in the back of your car?

Put him in the front.

Astronaut:
Doctor, I keep dreaming that there are huge, ugly aliens playing tiddlywinks under my bed. What shall I do?

Doctor: Hide the tiddlywinks.

What's the name of the first satellite that orbited Earth?

The moon.

What do you call an overweight ET?

An extra cholesterol.

Astronaut: I once lived on water for eight months.

Reporter: Goodness, when was that?

Astronaut: When I was in the navy.

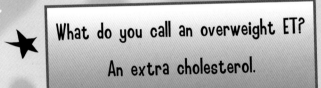

What did Neptune say to Saturn?

Give me a ring sometime.

How far can you see on a clear day?

93 million miles - from here to the sun.

What sea is in space?

The galax-sea!

Have you heard that scientists have found life on another planet?

Really?

Yes, they found fleas on Pluto!

Did you hear about the astronaut who stepped on chewing gum?

He got stuck in Orbit!

When do aliens eat eyeballs?

On fried-eyes.

What do you do with a blue Martian?

Try to cheer him up.

What happened to Ray when he met the man-eating alien?

He became ex-Ray.

What do you get if you cross
an alien with a dog?

A neighbourhood without cats.

What does one star
say to another star?

Glad to meteor.

Alien 1: Have you ever tasted the sun?

Alien 2: No, but I've heard it's outta
this world!

What do
moon people do
when they get married?

They go off on their
honeyearth!

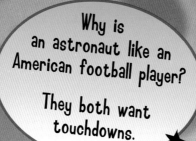

Why is an astronaut like an American football player?

They both want touchdowns.

What is an astronomical unit?

A heck of a big apartment.

Life on Earth is expensive but you get an annual free trip around the sun.

What food should you eat in space?

Nep-tuna.

What do you call ants in space?

Cosmonants & Astronants.

Astronaut: Doctor, the chemist said that these pills you prescribed me are for cows.

Doctor: Well, you said you wanted to be as strong as an ox.

How do you make an alien burn her ear?

Ring her up when she's ironing.

Why did the astronaut put sugar on his pillow?

So he could have sweet dreams.

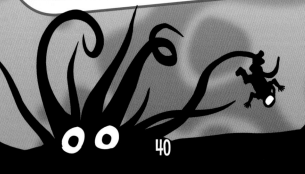

Where did the alien
keep his money?

Aliens don't need money.

Astronaut:
Doctor, how can I lose
15 kilos of fat?

Doctor: Try cutting
your head off.

Astronaut: Doctor, I think I'm
turning into a mummy.

Doctor: Better keep well wrapped up then.

Astronaut:
Doctor, what did the x-ray of
my head show?

Doctor: Absolutely nothing.

Astronaut: Waiter! Is this a chicken or beef pie?

Waiter: What did you order, sir?

Why did the Martian grab a bar of soap when his spaceship landed in the sea?

He thought he could wash himself ashore.

Did you hear about the astronaut who dreamt he was eating a big marshmallow?

When he woke up in the morning his pillow had gone.

How do Martians cover cushions?

They sit on them.

Astronaut: Doctor, I feel like a mirror.

Doctor: Keep still, I'm combing my hair.

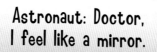

Astronaut: Doctor, I think I'm turning into a bee.

Doctor: Buzz off will you? I'm busy.

Astronaut: Doctor, everyone keeps ignoring me.

Doctor: Next please!

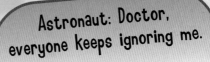

Astronaut: Doctor, I feel like a pair of curtains.

Doctor: Pull yourself together.

Astronaut:
Doctor, I've got wind.

Doctor: Buy yourself
a kite.

Astronaut: Doctor, I've got flat feet.

Doctor: Get a foot pump then.

Astronaut: Doctor, I
can't get to sleep at night.

Doctor: Lie on the end of the bed
and you'll soon drop off.

Why did
Mickey Mouse go up
into space?

To find Pluto.

Why are astronauts successful people?
Because they always go up in the world.

Astronaut:
Doctor, I feel like an apple.

Doctor: We must get to
the core of this.

What do you get if you cross a
rocket with a kangaroo?

A space shuttle that does short hops.

What do spacemen play football on?

Astro-turf.

What goes red, green, red, green, red, green?

A Martian in a liquidiser.

Astronaut: Doctor, I keep thinking I'm a snooker ball.

Doctor: Take your place at the back of the queue.

Astronaut: Doctor, I've only got fifty-nine seconds to live.

Doctor: I'll see you in a minute.

What's green and fast?

A Martian on roller skates.

Why did the spaceman throw the clock out of the window?

He wanted to see time fly.

Did you hear about the Martian who bought a sleeping bag?

He spent two months trying to wake it up.

What happened to the Martian who swallowed an oxo cube?

He made a laughing stock of himself.

Why did the astronaut take a ruler to bed with him?

So he could measure how long he slept.

What did
the alien say when he
landed in the forest?

Take me to your cedar.

What's green, has two antennae
and counts to ten backwards?

A Martian with the hiccups.

What kind of umbrella do
astronomers use in heavy rain?

A very wet one.

What did
the dog say to the Martian?

Woof! Woof!

How do you get a Martian into a matchbox?

Take out the matches first.

What did the hungry astronaut say when he only had thistles to eat?

Thistle have to do.

Why did the astronaut jump up and down?

He'd forgotten to shake his medicine.

Did you hear about the astronaut who jumped into the river in Paris?

The police said he was in-Seine.

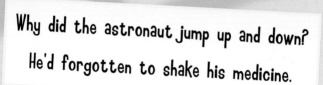

Astronaut: Waiter, this egg tastes off.

Waiter: Don't blame me sir, I only laid the table.

What happened when the silly alien went to a mind-reader?

She gave him his money back.

What do you call a Martian wearing ear muffs?

Whatever you want, he can't hear you.

How do you know there's a Martian in your bed?

Because he has an M on his pyjamas.

What kind of bandage do astronauts wear after heart surgery?

Ticker tape.

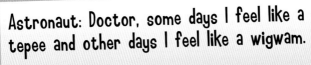

Astronaut: Doctor, some days I feel like a tepee and other days I feel like a wigwam.

Doctor: You're too tense.

Astronaut: Doctor, I keep thinking I'm a mosquito.

Doctor: Go away, sucker!

Astronaut: Doctor, my kidneys are bad. What should I do?

Doctor: Take them back to the butcher.

Astronaut: Doctor, will this ointment clear my spots?

Doctor: I never make rash promises.

Astronaut: Doctor, I've just swallowed a spoon.

Doctor: Sit there quietly and don't stir.

Astronaut: Doctor, I keep thinking I'm a roll of film.

Doctor: Don't worry, I'm sure nothing will develop.

Astronaut: Doctor, I keep painting myself gold.

Doctor: Don't worry, it's a gilt complex.

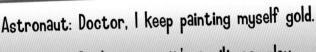

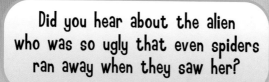

Astronaut:
Doctor, I've broken my
arm in two places.

Doctor: Well, don't go back
to them again.

Did you hear about the alien
who was so ugly that even spiders
ran away when they saw her?

What do aliens call baby whales?

Little squirts.

What is
green, wears dark
glasses and carries a pile
of exercise books?

A Martian disguised as
a teacher.

How can
you tell if an
astronaut is in a hurry?

He runs at
great space.

Astronaut: Waiter, there's a
maggot in my soup.

Waiter: Don't worry, sir, it
won't live long in that stuff.

Why did the astronaut put a
shoe by his ear?

He wanted to listen to sole music.

Why did the astronaut have
butterflies in his stomach?

Because he swallowed a caterpillar.

If a Martian was knocked out by Dracula in a fight, what would he be?

Out for the Count.

Why did the astronaut cross a wireless with a hairdresser?

He wanted to get radio waves.

What would you get if you crossed a Martian with a snail?

I don't know but it would slow him down a bit.

Astronaut: Doctor, I keep thinking there's two of me.

Doctor: One at a time, please.

What do you do if you find a Martian in your bed?

Sleep somewhere else.

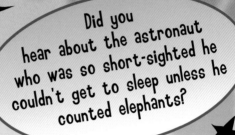

Did you hear about the astronaut who was so short-sighted he couldn't get to sleep unless he counted elephants?

Did you hear about the astronaut who put on a clean pair of socks every day?

By the end of the week he couldn't get his shoes on.

Astronaut: Waiter, this bread's got sand in it.

Waiter: That's to stop the butter slipping off.

Astronaut: Waiter, is there soup on the menu?

Waiter: No, I've wiped it off.

Astronaut: Waiter, what's this in my soup?

Waiter: I don't know sir, all insects look the same to me.

Astronaut: Waiter, do I have to sit here until I die of starvation?

Waiter: No, sir, we close at seven.

Astronaut: Doctor, I feel like a pin.

Doctor: I see your point.

Astronaut: Doctor, I keep thinking I'm a spider.

Doctor: What a web of lies.

Astronaut: Doctor, I keep thinking I'm a vampire.

Doctor: Necks, please.

Astronaut: Doctor, I feel like a yo-yo.

Doctor: Sit down…. sit down… sit down.

Astronaut: Doctor, everyone thinks I'm a liar.

Doctor: I can't believe that.

Astronaut: I keep thinking I'm a moth.

Doctor: Get out of my light!

What do you call an alien who swings from planet to planet?

Starzan.

Why is someone with rotten teeth like outer space?

Their teeth are full of black holes.

What did the alien say when he landed in the library?

Take me to your reader.

How did
the skeleton speak
to the Martian?

On a telebone.

What was written on the
hypochondriac astronaut's gravestone?

I told you I was ill!

What did the ghost say to
the astronaut as it floated
through the spaceship?

Don't worry, I'm just passing through!

What did the stupid alien call his pet tiger?

Spot.

Why did the astronaut decide to become an electrician?

To get a little light relief.

How did the astronaut feel when he got a big bill from the electricity company?

A bit shocked.

How did the alien get an electric shock?

He stood on a bun and a current ran up his leg.

Why did the alien want to work in a bank?

He was told there was money in it.

Why did the lazy alien get a job in a bakery?

He wanted a good loaf.

Did you hear about the alien that was a miracle worker?

It was a miracle when he worked.

How did the astronaut knit a suit of armour?

He used steel wool.

Why was the big, hairy, two-headed alien top of the class at school?

Because two heads are better than one.

What did the astronauts do when they had rock cakes for lunch?

Take their pick.

Alien: I've just swallowed a bone!

Friend: Are you serious?

Alien: No, I'm choking.

Why did the other kids call Bill a space cadet?

Because he had a lot of space between his ears.

Why couldn't the aliens play badminton?

Because they couldn't find a space shuttle.

Alien
(playing football): Why
didn't you stop the ball?

Friend: I thought that was what
the net was for.

What can an astronaut keep
and give away at the same time?

A cold.

Why did the astronaut eat six dinners?

He wanted to be a big success.

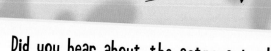

Did you hear about the astronaut who
was so old that when he went to school
history was called current events.

Martian to son: I taught you everything I know and still you're ignorant!

What's the difference between a Martian and an elephant?

Quite a lot, really.

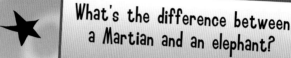

What did the alien say to the flea?

Stop bugging me.

What's worse for an astronaut than finding a maggot in his apple?

Finding half a maggot.

What did the alien say when he met a toad?

Wart's new?

What did the astronaut do when he found a bookworm chewing his log book?

Took the words right out of his mouth.

What do you call an alien with a frog on her head?

Lily.

Why did the astronaut use stones to stop moths eating his spacesuit?

Because a rolling stone gathers no moths.

Why did the bored alien
nibble a hole in the carpet?

He wanted to see the floor show.

Why do baby Martians like cobras?

Because they come with their own rattle.

Which hand would you
use to grab a fierce alien?

Your enemy's.

Why wouldn't the alien go on the
speak your weight machine?

He had his own scales.

What do you do if you find an alien in your bathroom?

Wait until he's finished.

Did you hear the joke about the slippery alien?

You wouldn't grasp it.

How do aliens get milk from cats?

Steal their saucers.

Who are the aliens' all-time favourite popstars?

The Space Girls!

Where does a ten-tonne Martian sleep?

Anywhere it wants to.

Why did the alien go on a diet?

It weighed too much for its scales.

What's green and goes round and round at 60 miles an hour?

A Martian in a blender.

Now you see it... now you don't. What are you looking at?

A black alien walking across a zebra crossing.

What do you get if you cross a fierce alien with a frog?

A creature that can bite you from the other side of the road.

What do you call an alien with no legs?

Anything you like - it won't be able to chase you.

Why did the astronaut marry the cleaner?

Because she swept him right off his feet.

What do you get if you cross an alien with a hyena?

I don't know, but if it laughs, join in.

What is Zog the Martian's middle name?

The.

What do you get if you cross a three-headed alien with a skunk?

A very ugly smell.

What did the alien do when his tail was cut off?

He went to the re-tail shop.

What do you get if you cross a Martian with a cow?

Milk shakes that are out of this world.

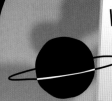

What did the grape do when the fat alien sat on it?

It let out a little wine.

Why did the astronaut take a load of hay to bed?

To feed his nightmare.

What did the Martian say when he was asked if he wanted a duck egg for tea?

Only if you quack it for me.

If twenty aliens run after one alien what time is it?

Twenty after one.

How does a big, fat alien go up a tree?

He stands on an acorn and waits for it to grow.

What do Martians use cowhide for?

To hold cows together.

There were ten astronauts in a spaceship. All but nine jumped out. How many were left?

Nine.

What do you get if you cross an alien with a flower?

I don't know but I'm not going to smell it.

What's green and smells?

A Martian's nose.

Did you hear about the mean astronaut?

When he found a crutch he broke his leg so that he could use it.

Did you hear about the red-headed alien?

No hair, just a red head.

Astronaut: I'm suffering from bad breath.

Friend: You should do something about it.

Astronaut: I am, I've just sent my wife to the dentist.

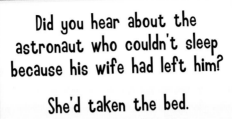

Did you hear about the astronaut who couldn't sleep because his wife had left him?

She'd taken the bed.

Little alien: Mummy, mummy why do you keep poking Daddy in the ribs?

Mummy alien: If I don't the fire will go out.

Where do aliens play golf?

On the 18 black hole golf course.

Did you hear about the big-headed Martian who was looking for a wife?

He couldn't find anyone to love him as much as he loved himself.

Alien boy: What would it take to make you give me a kiss?

Alien girl: An anaesthetic.

What should an astronaut do before going on a long journey?

Planet carefully!

Astronaut: Doctor, I keep thinking I'm a squirrel.

Doctor: Oh no, another nutcase!

Astronaut: Doctor, I keep thinking I'm a door.

Doctor: Let me know when you're unhinged.

Astronaut: Doctor, how can I avoid falling hair?

Doctor: Step to one side.

Astronaut: Doctor, this banana diet isn't working.

Doctor: Stop scratching and come down from the curtains.

Did you hear about the alien who'd been asked to get married hundreds of times?

Really? Who by?

Her parents.

Did you hear about the alien who was so dim he thought a cartoon was a song you sing in the car?

Alien: Have you ever seen anyone who looks like me before?

Girl: Yes, but I had to pay admission.

Did you hear about the astronaut who was ashamed of his long black hair?

He always wore long gloves to cover up his hands.

Did you hear about the girl who got engaged to an astronaut then found out he had a wooden leg?

She broke it off, of course!

Did you hear about the alien who did a four-year course in ugliness?

He finished it in two.

Why did the alien wear a
turtleneck sweater?

To cover his flea collar.

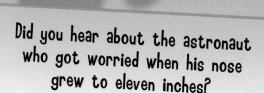

Did you hear about the astronaut
who got worried when his nose
grew to eleven inches?

He thought it might turn into a foot.

Why did the alien have
her hair in a bun?

Because she had her nose in a hamburger.

Did you hear about Britain's
oldest astronaut. She's 115 years old
and hasn't got a single grey hair.

She's completely bald.

Did you hear about the astronaut who was so fat when he got on a speak your weight machine it surrendered.

Did you hear about the astronaut who was so small his chin had a rash from his bootlaces?

Did you hear about the astronaut who had his trousers made from sun-blind material?

Every time the sun came out, his trousers rolled down.

Did you hear about the astronaut who was so fat his wife had to stand up in bed each morning to see if it was daylight?

Did you hear about the silly alien who tried to make a birthday cake?

The candles melted in the oven.

Did you hear about the astronaut who spent a fortune on deodorants before he found out that people didn't like him anyway?

What's green and goes beep, beep?

A Martian in a traffic jam.

Why did the alien plant bulbs in his garden?

So the worms could see where they were going.

What's the best thing
to give a seasick alien?

Plenty of room.

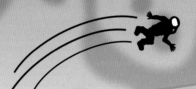

What happened to the cow
after he jumped over the moon?

He was stolen by a beefburglar.

What do you call an alien
with a seagull on his head?

Cliff.

What did the silly alien do when
he found a flea in his ear?

Shoot it.

What do you call an alien
with a spade on his head?

Doug.

What's green and coughs?

A Martian with a cold.

What's the best way
to stop an alien from sliding
through the eye of a needle?

Tie a knot in its neck.

Did you hear what happened to the
silly alien who had a brain transplant?

The brain rejected him.

What did the alien say when he landed in the jungle?

Take me to your lemur.

Did you hear about the alien who couldn't stop eating cream buns?

She was thick to her stomach.

Did you hear about the alien who didn't like soup?

He couldn't get it to stay on his fork.

What do you call an alien who's always around when you want him?

Andy.

What did the Martian do when he split his sides laughing?

Ran until he got a stitch.

What happened when the Martians played tennis with a bad egg?

First it went ping, then it went pong.

Did you hear about the alien who was so ugly he could make his own yoghurt by staring at a pint of milk for an hour?

Why did the alien plant coins in his garden?

He wanted to raise some cash.

What did the astronaut take when he was run down?

The number of the car that hit him.

Did you hear about the alien who went on a crash diet?

Now he looks a wreck.

Did you hear about the alien whose mouth is so big he can sing a duet all by himself?

Did you hear about the silly alien who made his chickens drink hot water?

He thought they would lay hard-boiled eggs.

How did the stupid astronaut cure his headache?

He put his head through the window and the pane disappeared.

Did you hear about the fat alien who was on a seafood diet?

The more he saw food the more he ate.

Did you hear about the alien who was so ugly that when a wasp stung her it shut its eyes?

What do you call an alien who doesn't like butter?

Marge.

What do you call an alien with one leg shorter than the other?

Eileen.

Did you hear about the alien who was so fat he could sit around a table all by himself?

Did you hear about the astronaut whose teeth were like stars?

They came out at night.

Alien 1: I hear that Zog is going places.

Alien 2: The sooner the better.

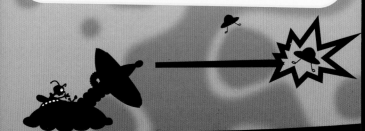

Did you hear about
the alien who wanted to go
water-skiing but couldn't find
a sloping lake?

What kind of tree would you
find in an alien's kitchen?

A pan-try!

Did you hear about the alien
who was as pretty as a flower?

A cauliflower.

Did you
hear about the alien
who sat under a cow?

He got a pat on
the head.

What is green all over
but has a red face?

A Martian with sunburn.

Did you
hear about the alien that
was so cold-blooded when a
mosquito bit him it got
pneumonia?

Why did the stupid astronaut
have a horse on her head?

She wanted a ponytail.

Did you hear about the Martian
who was like an oil well?

He was always boring.

What do you call an alien with a hat full of cement?

A blockhead.

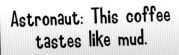

Astronaut: This coffee tastes like mud.

Waitress: It was only ground this morning.

Why did the Martian eat the candle?

He wanted a light snack.

Why did the silly alien throw away his guitar?

Because it had a hole in it.

Where does the president of Mars live?

In the greenhouse.

What happens to aliens who eat yeast and shoe polish?

They rise and shine in the morning.

Did you hear the joke about the empty spaceship?

There's nothing in it.

Why did the astronaut wear brown boots?

His black ones were at the menders.

Astronaut:
Doctor, how can I avoid this run down feeling?

Doctor: Try looking both ways when you cross the road.

Astronaut: Doctor, I feel like a racehorse.

Doctor: Take one of these every four laps.

What do you call an alien with a wooden head?

Edward.

Astronaut: Doctor, I'm boiling up!

Doctor: Just simmer down.

Why are Martian
schools held in
flying saucers?

So the pupils can get a
higher education.

What looks
like half a Martian?

The other half.

How did the Martian keep
cool at the football match?

He sat by a fan.

How do you keep a sweaty
Martian from smelling?

Cut off his nose.

Did you hear about the alien who was so ugly his parents ran away from home?

How do Martians communicate with fish?

They drop them a line.

Did you hear about the astronaut whose teeth stuck out so much it looked like his nose was playing a piano?

Astronaut: Doctor, I keep thinking I'm a guitar.

Doctor: You are highly strung!

Astronaut: Doctor, I feel like a banana.

Doctor: Well, your skin is peeling.

Astronaut: Doctor, how can I stop my hair getting thinner?

Doctor: Why do you want fat hair?

Astronaut: Doctor, I feel like I'm going bald.

Doctor: You need some fresh 'air.

What do you call the moon after a huge feast?

A full moon.

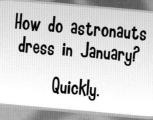

How do astronauts dress in January?

Quickly.

What do you call an alien with a cat on her head?

Kitty.

Did you hear about the astronaut with a two-foot beard?

He walked on his chin.

Did you hear about the alien who was so ugly he had to keep buying a new mirror?

What happened
to the alien who
pinched a bar of soap?

He made a clean
getaway.

Why did the alien
take a pencil to bed?

To draw the curtains.

Why didn't the Martian starve at the seaside?

Because of the sand which is there.

Where was the astronaut
when the lights went out?

In the dark.

What do astronauts like to put in a pie?

Their teeth.

Why can't an alien's head be twelve inches wide?

Because if it was it would be a foot.

What did the Martian do when her baby swallowed a biro?

Use a pencil.

What's green, has two antennae and a trunk?

A Martian going on holiday.

How did the sailor know there was a man in the moon?

He went to sea.

What did the alien give to his auntie who had a sore throat?

Aunti-septic.

Alien: You're so ugly your face would stop a clock!

Friend: And yours would make one run.

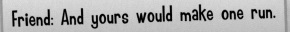

Alien: Don't you think my little girl has grown.

Friend: Yes, she's certainly gruesome.

Why did the Martian buy
some clothes?

Because he couldn't get
them for nothing.

Why did the alien comb
his hair with his toes?

To make ends meet.

Why did
the Martian
have sideburns?

His electric blanket
was too hot.

Why did the Martian wear
his socks inside out?

Because there were holes
on the other side.

How did
the astronaut stop moles
from digging up his garden?

He took away their spade.

Why did the alien laugh at the owl?

Because he was such a hoot.

Why couldn't the astronaut
send an e-mail to the orange?

The lime was engaged.

Two Martians landed their
spaceship by a traffic light.

I saw her first, said one Martian.

So what? said the other.
I'm the one she winked at.

Astronaut: Waiter, there's a dead fly in my soup.

Waiter: Yes, sir, it's the heat that kills them.

Astronaut: Waiter, this lemonade is cloudy.
Waiter: No sir, it's the glass that's dirty.

Astronaut: Waiter, there's a frog in my soup.

Waiter: Sorry, sir, the flies are on holiday.

Astronaut: Waiter, this chicken soup has dots in it.

Waiter: It's okay sir, it's only chickenpox.

What did the astronaut
do when his budgie escaped?

Called the Flying Squad.

How do you make an alien stew?

Make it wait for hours.

What goes
UG! UG! Bonk!

An alien laughing his
head off.

Why did the alien take a ladder to the party?

Because the drinks were on the house.

Why did
the Martian cross the road?

Because his spaceship was on
the other side.

What do you call an alien
floating on a raft in the sea?

Bob.

How do you hire a spaceship?

Put bricks under it.

Why is an alien easy to weigh?

Because he has his own scales.

How does
the moon cut its hair?

E-clipse it.

What do you call an alien
in a jumbo jet?

A passenger.

What do you get if you cross
an alien with a parrot?

I don't know but if it says
Pretty Polly smile!

What was the alien doing in the rain?

Getting wet.

Astronaut: Waiter, I asked for a three-course meal.

Waiter: That's what you've got sir - two chips and a pea.

Astronaut: Waiter, there's a hair in my honey.

Waiter: It must have dropped off the comb, sir.

Astronaut: Waiter, there's a button in my soup.

Waiter: It must have fallen off when the salad was dressing.

Astronaut: Waiter, this bun tastes like soap.

Waiter: It's a bath-bun sir.

One Martian to another: I'm sorry but I just don't believe there's life on Earth.

Where did the astronaut go when he caught laryngitis?

To the croakroom.

Where do astronauts with no hair live?

In Baldimore.

What do you get if you cross a slimy alien with a shopper?

A slippery customer.

What did
the alien get when
he crossed a glow-worm
with a python?

A twenty-foot strip
light that squeezed
him to death.

Why did the Martian wear
a belt on his teeth?

He couldn't find his braces.

What did the alien get when he
crossed an electric eel with a sponge?

A shock absorber.

What did the alien get when he
crossed a snake with a Lego set?

A boa constructor.

Why did the astronaut feed his cat with pennies?

He wanted to put them in the kitty.

What did the alien get when he crossed a sheep and a rainstorm?

A wet blanket.

What do you get if you cross a giant alien with a blackbird?

A lot of broken telephone poles.

What did the astronaut's budgie say when it laid a square egg?

Ouch!

What did the alien get when he crossed a chicken with a cow?

Roost beef.

What happened when the alien threw a green stone in the Red Sea?

It got wet.

What's the name of the Dog Star?

Lassie.

If there were five flies on a Martian's dinner and he hit one of them how many would be left?

Just the squashed one.

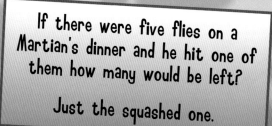

Why does E.T.
have such big eyes?

Have you seen the size
of his phone bill?

If athletes
get athlete's foot
what do astronauts get?

Missile toe.

What's green and goes
boing-boing-boing!

A Martian on a pogo stick.

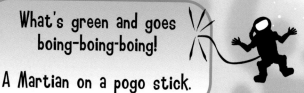

Astronaut: Doctor, I think I'm a bell.

Doctor: Take this medicine. If it
doesn't help give me a ring.

Astronaut: Doctor, I can't stop my hand shaking.

Doctor: Do you drink a lot?

Astronaut: No, I spill most of it.

Astronaut: Doctor, I keep getting pains in the eye when I drink coffee.

Doctor: Have you tried taking the spoon out of the cup?

Astronaut: Doctor, I've just swallowed a pen.

Doctor: Well, sit down and write your name.

Astronaut: Doctor, I feel like a dog.

Doctor: Sit!

Astronaut: Doctor, I feel like a spoon.

Doctor: Well, sit still and don't stir.

Astronaut: Doctor, I feel like a pack of cards.

Doctor: I'll deal with you later.

Why did the astronaut take a glow-worm on board his spaceship?

To lighten it.

Why don't Martians keep chickens as pets?

They don't want their children to hear fowl language.

How did the fat alien get down from the tree?

He sat on a leaf and waited for autumn.

What fish do Martians eat with chips?

Starfish.

Why did the alien feed money to the cow?

He fancied some rich milk.

Why did the Martian paint his toenails red?

So he could hide in the cherry tree.

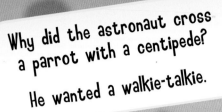

Why did the astronaut cross a parrot with a centipede?

He wanted a walkie-talkie.

What do you get if you cross an alien with a boy scout?

A creature that scares old ladies across the road.

What is ugly, scary and very blue?

An alien holding its breath.

What's green with red spots?

A Martian with measles.

What time is it when an alien comes to dinner?

Time to go.

How did the Martian make fruit punch?

He gave it boxing lessons.

Why did the Martian scratch himself?

Because no one else knew where he itched.

What's yellow on the outside and green on the inside?

A Martian disguised as a banana.

How do Martians keep flies out of their kitchen?

They put a bucket of manure in the living room.

Why did the astronaut take an aspirin when he heard the werewolf howl?

Because it gave him an eerie ache.

What did the Sun say to the moon?

Don't you think I look hot?

What did the alien's mother say when the young alien chased an astronaut around a tree?

Don't play with your food.

Why did the astronaut feed his chickens whisky?

He wanted scotch eggs.

How do aliens make milk shake?

They give it a good scare.

Did you hear about the astronaut who hit his head?

He saw stars!

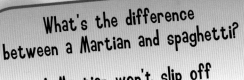

What's the difference between a Martian and spaghetti?

A Martian won't slip off the end of your fork.

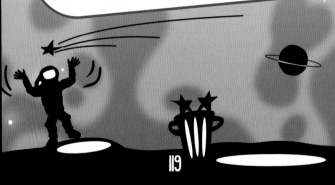

Two aliens wandered into a games arcade. Goodness, said one, staring around in amazement. People here feed the creatures with metal discs!

Why did the Martian walk into the building?

Because he didn't see it.

What illness do retired astronauts get?

Flew.

What did the little star say to the big star?

You're too young to be out at night.

Why did
the astronaut call
his dog Camera?

Because he was
always snapping.

What's the same size as an
alien but weighs nothing?

Its shadow.

Why are aliens easy to fool?

They'll swallow anything.

Did you
hear about the alien
who bought a paper shop?

It blew away.

What flowers
do astronauts grow
under their noses?

Tulips.

What would you get if you crossed
a Martian with a kangaroo?

Australia would be full of craters.

What's green and jumps up and down?

A Martian on a trampoline.

What do
aliens use to keep
their hair in place?

Scare spray.

How do aliens
count to 100?

On their fingers.

Why do aliens tickle you
before they eat you?

They want a happy meal.

Why don't aliens eat clowns?

Because they taste funny.

What did the horse say to the Martian?

Nothing. Horses don't talk.

Why did the Martian
invite the mushroom to his party?

Because he was a fungi.

Six Martians were standing
under an umbrella. How come
they didn't get wet?

It wasn't raining.

What do you call a deaf alien?

Anything you like, he can't hear you.

How did the teacher know that
Molly was going to be an astronaut
when she grew up?

She took up so much space at school.

Why did the Martian plant gold in his garden?

He wanted rich soil.

What happened to the Martian when he crossed an electric blanket with a toaster?

He kept popping out of bed in the morning.

How did the moon fall down?

Through one of the black holes.

Why was the Martian staring at the car radio?

He wanted to see a car-toon.

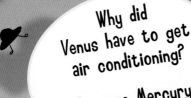

Why did
Venus have to get
air conditioning?

Because Mercury
moved in.

How do you save a Martian from
drowning in hot chocolate?

Throw him a marshmallow.

What was the first animal in space?

The cow that jumped over the moon.

What can an astronaut
hold in their right hand but
not in their left hand?

Their left elbow.

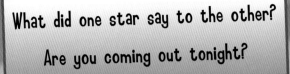

What did one star say to the other?

Are you coming out tonight?

Why did the astronaut put his dog in the shade?

Because he didn't fancy a hot dog.

Why did Uranus move?

Because Saturn was too bright.

Why did the astronaut throw the lettuce out of the window?

Because she wanted a tossed salad.

What has
handles and flies?

An alien in a dustbin.

Why didn't the astronaut
get his hair wet in the shower?

He was bald.

How did the Martian feel
after he was run over by a car?

Tyred.

How can you help starving aliens?

Give them a hand.

Why shouldn't
you grab an alien by its tail?

It might be the alien's tail but it
could be the end of you.

What illness did
everyone on the Starship
Enterprise catch?

Chicken Spocks.

Why did the alien stand on his head?

His feet were tired.

What did the Martian say when
his wife fell down the wishing well?

It works.

What did the alien say
to the window cleaner?

Take me to your ladder.

What did E.T's mum say when he got home?

Where on earth have you been?

What did
the alien say to the dog?

Take me to your breeder.

What is a light year?

The same as a normal year
but with less calories.

What did the alien say
to the cat?

Take me to your litter.

What do you get if you cross
a giant alien with a penguin?

I don't know but it's a very
tight-fitting dinner suit.

How can
you tell the
difference between a rabbit
and a Martian?

Try getting a Martian
into a hutch.

What's huge, ugly, dangerous
and has 16 wheels?

An alien on roller skates.

Why don't Martians use toothpaste?

Because their teeth aren't loose.

How do you greet a three-headed alien?

Hello, hello, hello.

How did the Martian lose his hair?

In a hair raid.

Did you hear about the alien who flew a spaceship from Neptune to Uranus in just 3 minutes and 21 seconds?

He's listed in the Guinness Book Of Out-Of-This-World Records

How do
aliens like their eggs?

Terror-fried.

Where do Martians get their eggs?

From the little green hen.

Why do aliens eat raw meat?

Because they don't know how to cook.

What sort
of soup do aliens like?

One with plenty of body
in it.

Why don't aliens celebrate Christmas?

Because they don't like to give away their presence.

What's the difference between an alien and sunset?

A sunset is beautiful.

Did you hear about the Martian who had a face like a million dollars?

Green and wrinkled.

Why are aliens messy tea-drinkers?

With flying saucers, it's hard not to spill it.

What did the alien say to
the fat astronaut?

Take me to your feeder.

Did you hear about the astronaut
who took lots of exercise?

He was very long-winded.

Why did
the astronaut
hit the clock?

Because the clock
struck first.

Why is an alien like
uncultivated woodland?

They are both totally dense.

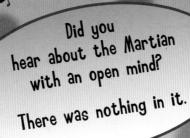

Did you hear about the Martian with an open mind?

There was nothing in it.

Did you hear about the astronaut who was always flying off the handle?

He had a screw loose.

Why did the alien sleep under the car?

He wanted to wake up oily the next morning.

What's brown, white and yellow and travels at 1,000,000,000 miles a hour?

An astronaut's egg sandwich.

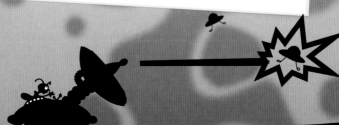

When is an alien like a
bowl of custard?

When he's yellow and thick.

Why did the Martian stand on
the roof to sing?

So he could reach the high notes.

How do you make a Martian smart?

Squirt lemon juice in his eye.

Why did
the Martian stop
making doughnuts?

He was sick of the
whole business.

What's the difference between an alien and gravy?

Gravy's only thick some of the time.

Astronaut: Waiter, this food isn't fit for a pig.

Waiter: I'll bring you some that is, sir.

Waiter: Did you enjoy the cottage pie, sir?

Astronaut: No, it tastes like you've left the drains in it.

Astronaut: Waiter, I'll have soup and fish, please.

Waiter: I'd have the fish first, sir, it's just on the turn.

Astronaut: Waiter, this coffee tastes like soap.

Waiter: That must be the tea, sir - the coffee tastes like mud.

What did the alien do when the doctor said he had rabies?

Wrote a list of the people he wanted to bite.

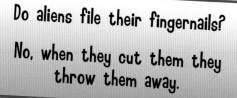

Do aliens file their fingernails?

No, when they cut them they throw them away.

How do Martians get to sleep?

By counting stars.

Why did the alien throw a
bucket of water out of the window?

He wanted to make a big splash.

Why did
the astronaut leave
his watch at home when
he went on the spaceship?

Because time
flies anyway.

Astronaut: Doctor, can you help me out?

Doctor: Certainly, sir, which way did you
come in?

Why did the astronaut put his
stereo in the fridge?

Because he wanted to listen to cool music.

Why is an alien like a collection of famous actors' autographs?

They've both come from the stars.

What did the banana do when the alien chased it?

The banana split.

When is an alien like a vampire?

When he's got bat breath.

Did you hear about the alien shoplifter?

He went around picking up shops.

What's green and squirts jam at you?

A Martian eating a doughnut.

An alien was lost in the forest. How did he send a message home?

By moss code.

Who's long, slippery, and always phones home when he goes sightseeing?

E.T. the extra tourist eel.

Where did the Martian go to pick up some bees?

To the buzz stop.

What happened to the alien's cat when she swallowed some wool?

She had mittens.

Why did the alien drag a cabbage on a lead?

He thought it was a cauli.

Why do stupid aliens eat biscuits?

Because they're crackers.

Why did the silly astronaut wear all his clothes to paint his spaceship?

Because it said on the tin: Put on at least three coats.

What sort of children does an alien florist have?

Bloomin' idiots.

What followed the alien?

Its tail.

What did the alien find in the middle of the jellyfish?

A jelly button.

Astronaut: Doctor, have you got something for a bad headache?

Doctor: Here, hit yourself over the head with this hammer, that'll give you a bad headache!